Text Formatting
Easy Word Essentials
Volume 1

M.L. HUMPHREY

TITLES BY M.L. HUMPHREY

EASY WORD ESSENTIALS
Text Formatting
Page Formatting
Lists
Tables
Track Changes

WORD ESSENTIALS
Word for Beginners
Intermediate Word

MAIL MERGE ESSENTIALS
Mail Merge for Beginners

CONTENTS

INTRODUCTION

In *Word for Beginners* I covered the basics of working in Word and in *Intermediate Word* I covered more intermediate-level topics. But I realized that some users will just want to know about a specific topic and not buy a guide that covers a variety of other topics that aren't of interest to them.

So this series of guides is meant to address that need. Each guide in the series covers one specific topic such as formatting, tables, or track changes.

I'm going to assume in these guides that you have a basic understanding of how to navigate Word, although each guide does include an Appendix with a brief discussion of basic terminology to make sure that we're on the same page.

The guides are written using Word 2013, which should be similar enough for most users of Word to follow, but anyone using a version of Word prior to Word 2007 probably won't be able to use them effectively.

Also, keep in mind that the content in these guides is drawn from *Word for Beginners* and *Intermediate Word*, so if you think you'll end up buying all of these guides you're probably better off just buying *Word for Beginners* and *Intermediate Word* instead.

Having said all of that, let's talk text and paragraph formatting, including how to use Styles and the Format Painter.

TEXT FORMATTING

Once you type your text into your document, chances are you'll want to format it in some way by either changing the font or the font size or the color or any of a number of attributes. In this section we'll discuss how to format text.

CHOOSING A FONT – GENERAL THOUGHTS

The font you use governs the general appearance of the text in your document. My version of Word uses Calibri font as the default, but there are hundreds of fonts you can choose. Here is a sample of a few of those choices:

Sans-Serif Examples:
Calibri
Arial
Gill Sans MT

> **Serif Font Examples:**
>
> Times New Roman
>
> Garamond
>
> Palatino Linotype

The first three samples are sans-serif fonts. (That just means they don't have little feet at the bottom of the letters.) The second three samples are serif fonts. (They do have those little feet at the bottom of each letter.) All of these fonts are the same size, but you can see that the different fonts have a different appearance and take up different amounts of space on the page. Arial is darker and taller than Calibri, for example.

Many companies and teachers will specify the font you need to use. If they don't I'd suggest using a serifed font like Garamond or Times New Roman for text since serifed fonts are supposed to be easier to read.

And unless you're working on a creative project, don't get too fancy with your fonts. The six listed in that example above should cover almost any text needs you have. At the end of the day, the goal is for someone to be able to read what you've written. So no Algerian in many body text. Save fonts like that for embellishments and section labels.

CHANGING THE FONT

There are a few ways you can change the font in your document. If you already know you want to use a different font, it's easiest to do so before you start typing. Otherwise you'll need to select all of the text you want to change. (Either with Select All if it's all text in the document or by selecting chunks of text and changing them one chunk at a time.)

The first way to change the font is to go to the Font section of the Home tab. Click on the arrow to the right of the current font name and choose from the dropdown menu.

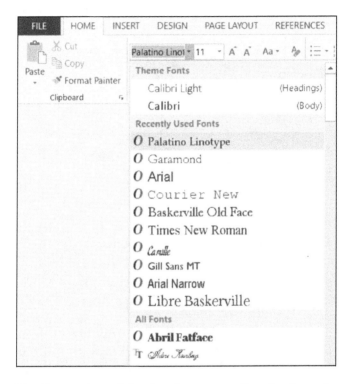

The first section of the dropdown menu lists the fonts for the theme you're using. Usually that'll be the defaults for Word, in this case, Calibri and Calibri Light. Next you'll see Recently Used Fonts. Most of the time there will only be one or two fonts here, but I had used a number recently.

Finally, you'll see a list of all available fonts in alphabetical order. If you know the font you want, you can start typing in its name rather than scroll through the entire list. Otherwise, use the scroll bar on the right-hand side to move through the list. Each font is written using the font to give you an idea what it will look like. See in the example the difference between Algerian and Garamond?

The next way to change your font is to right-click and choose Font from the dropdown menu. This will bring up the Font dialogue box. In the top left corner you can choose the font you want.

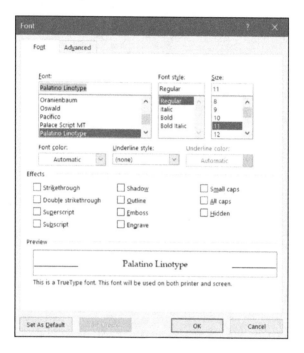

There's a third option for changing the font, something I'm going to call the mini formatting menu, in the newest versions of Word. To see this menu, right-click in your document or select a section of text using your mouse. When you select a section of text, a smaller version of the Font section of the Home tab will appear just above your text. If you right-click it will appear above the dropdown menu.

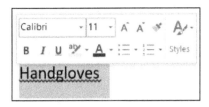

As you can see, one of the options that you can change in the mini formatting menu is the font. (If the font name box is empty, that's because you have text selected and there's more than one font in the selection.) To change the font, click on the arrow to the right of the listed font and choose the one you want from the dropdown just like you would in the Font section of the Home tab. I would recommend that you only use this option for a selection of text that you want to change to a new font. It's much better to change the font for your document in the Home tab.

FONT SIZE

Font size dictates how large the text will be. Here are some examples of different font sizes:

8 pt   12pt   16pt

As you can see, the larger the font size, the larger the text. Most documents are written in a ten, eleven, or twelve point font size. Often footnotes or endnotes will use eight or nine point. Chapter headings or title pages will use the larger font sizes. Whatever font size you do use, try to be consistent between different sections of your document. So all main body text should use just one font size. Same for chapter or section headings.

Changing the font size works much the same way as changing the font. You have the same three options: You can go to the Font section of the Home tab, bring up the mini formatting menu by right-clicking, or bring up the Font dialogue box by right-clicking and choosing Font from the dropdown menu. If you want to change existing text, you need to select the text first. If you want to change the font size for text that you're going to type, do so with the Home tab or the Font dialogue box options.

For all three options the font size is listed to the right of the font name.

For the Home tab or mini formatting menu options, you can click on the arrow next to the current font size to bring up a dropdown menu that lets you choose your font size. In the Font dialogue box that list of choices is already visible.

If the font size you want isn't listed, you can type it in instead. Just click into the box for font size and change the number to the font size you want to use.

In the Home tab and the mini formatting menu, if you're only changing the font by one or two point sizes, you can instead use the increase and decrease font options directly to the right of the font size. These are depicted as the letter A with a small arrow above it. The one on the left is an arrow that points upward (to increase the font size). The one on the right is an arrow that points downward (to decrease the font size). If you use the increase/decrease font options, they increase and decrease the font size one place according to the font sizes listed in the dropdown menu.

Here is an image of all three choices for changing font size in the Home tab.

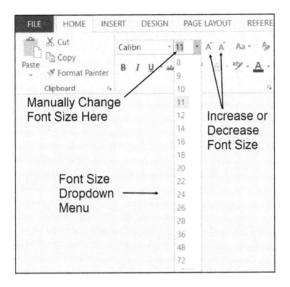

FONT COLOR

Changing your font color works the same as changing your font or font size. Select the text you want to change and then either go to the Font section of the Home tab, pull up the mini formatting menu, or right-click and choose Font from the dropdown menu to bring up the Font dialogue box. This time, though, you want to click on the arrow next to the A with the solid colored line under it in the bottom right corner of the section:

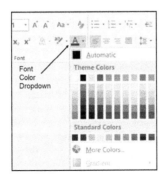

This will give you a dropdown menu with seventy different colors to choose from. Click on the color you want and it will change your text to that color.

If those seventy choices are not enough, you can click on More Colors at the bottom of the dropdown box. This will bring up the Colors dialogue box where you can choose from even more colors or specify a specific color in the Custom tab using RGB values.

HIGHLIGHTING TEXT

Another thing you can do is highlight text in a document much like you might do with a highlighter. You can do this from the Font section of the Home tab or in the mini formatting menu. Select the text you want to highlight and then look for the letters ab and what looks like a pen running diagonally right to left between the ab and a colored line:

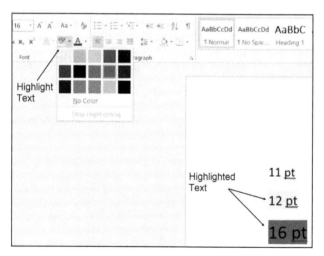

If you want to highlight using the color shown in the line, you can just click on the image. If you want to use a different color, left-click on the arrow and select your color from the dropdown menu.

If you ever highlight text and want to remove the highlight, you can do so by selecting that text, going to the highlight dropdown, and choosing the "no color" option.

Once you've used the highlighter it will show the last color you used as the default color until you close the file. (This carries across documents. I have three documents open at the moment and all three of them now show "no color" as the highlighter option even though I only used it in the one document.)

BOLDING TEXT

This is one you will use often. At least I do. The easiest way to bold text is to use Ctrl + B. You can use it before you start typing the text you want to bold or on a selection of text that you've chosen. For text that is already bolded, you can remove the bolding by selecting the text and using Ctrl + B as well. If you select text that is both bolded and not bolded, you'll need to type Ctrl + B twice, once to bold all of the text and once to remove it.

If you don't want to use the control keys, you can also go to the Font Section of the Home tab and click on the B on the left-hand side. It works the exact same way as using Ctrl + B. If you click on it and then type text that text will be bolded. Or you can select the text you want to bold and then click on the B. To turn off or remove bolding, click on the B again.

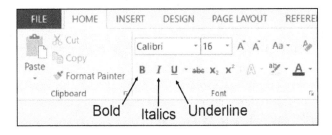

The final option is to select your text, right-click, choose Font from the dropdown menu, and then choose to Bold in the Font Style section of the Font dialogue box. (If you want to both bold and italicize text, you would choose Bold Italic.)

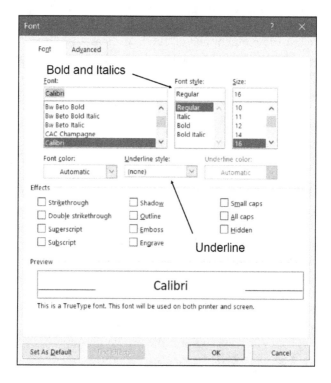

ITALICIZING TEXT

To place text into italics—that means to have it sloped to the side *like this*—the easiest way is to use Ctrl + I. It works the exact same way as bolding text. You can do it before you type the letters or select the text and then use it. And to remove italics, just select the text, and then type Ctrl + I until the italics are gone.

Or in the Font section of the Home tab, you can click on the slanted capital I. And if you use the Font dialogue box, italics are listed under Font Styles. (See the images above in the Bolding section.)

UNDERLINING TEXT

Underlining text works much the same way as bolding or italicizing text. The control keys you'll need to use are Ctrl + U and in the Font section of the Home tab the underline option is represented by an underlined U. (See image above in the Bolding section.)

Underline is different from italics and bold, though, because there are multiple underline options to choose from. Using Ctrl + U will provide a single line underline of your text. So will just clicking on the U in the Font section of the Home tab.

But if you click on the arrow next to the U in the Font section, you will see seven additional underline options you can choose from.

Choosing More Underlines at the bottom of that list of options will open the Font dialogue box where you will have a total of seventeen underline styles to choose from. You can also go direct to the Font dialogue box by selecting your text and then right-clicking and choosing Font from the dropdown. But, honestly, while it's good to know those other options are there the basic single underline will be all you need most of the time so if you remember anything remember Ctrl +U.

REMOVING BOLDING, UNDERLINING, OR ITALICS

I touched on this briefly above, but let's go over it again.

If you have bolded, underlined, or italicized text and you want to remove that formatting, you can simply select the text and use the command in question to remove that formatting type. So Ctrl + B, I, or U or click on the letter in the Font section of the Home tab or go to the Font dialogue box and remove the formatting from there.

If you select text that is partially formatted one way and partially formatted another—so say half of it is bolded and half is not—you may need to use the command twice. The first time will apply the formatting to all of the selected text, the second time will remove it from all of the selected text.

Also, with specialty underlining (all but the default, first choice), using Ctrl + U once will revert the type of underlining to the basic single underline. To remove the underline altogether, you'll need to use Ctrl + U a second time.

STRIKETHROUGH YOUR TEXT

If you ever want to keep text but place a line through the middle of it as if someone has come along and stricken it out, you can use strikethrough. To do so, select the text, go to the Font section of the Home tab, and choose the strikethrough option. It's the one with the letters abc with a line running through them just to the right of the underline option.

(Back in the good old days before track changes had really caught on, I worked with someone who showed their changes in a document this way. They'd use strikethrough to show the text they wanted deleted. Don't ever do that. Because if you do it that way someone is going to have to go through that document and manually delete all of your strikethroughs. That is not fun. If you run across a document where someone has done this, you can turn off strikethrough in the same way as you add it. Select the text and click on the strikethrough icon in the Font section of the Home tab.)

Another option for adding strikethrough is to select your text, right-click, choose Format from the dropdown, and then choose Strikethrough from the Effects section of the Font dialogue box. That approach also allows you to choose a double strikethrough option that puts two lines through the text instead of just one.

SUBSCRIPT OR SUPERSCRIPT YOUR TEXT

You may have painful flashbacks to math while we're talking about this and I apologize for that. A subscript is when you move the text so that it's lower than the rest of the text on the line and make it small. A superscript is when you move the text so that it's higher than the rest of the text on the line and also make it small. The best example of a superscript is the notation for a squared number. Remember three squared? It was written as 3^2?

If you ever need to do this (and I have needed to use superscripts when someone accidentally changed the formatting of all footnotes in a document to normal-size text), select the text you want to subscript or superscript and then go to the Font section of the Home tab. The two options are located just below where you choose the font size and just to the right of the strikethrough option. They're represented by a small bold x with a 2 in the subscript or superscript position, respectively. (Also, if you hold your mouse over each one, Word will tell you what they are and what they do.)

You can also access the subscript or superscript options by selecting your text, right-clicking, and choosing Font from the dropdown menu to bring up the Font dialogue box. The subscript and superscript options are in the Effects section of the Font tab.

They also have Ctrl shortcuts. Subscript is Ctrl + = and superscript is Ctrl + Shift + +. (That second one is holding down the control key, the shift key, and the + key all at the same time.)

PARAGRAPH FORMATTING

That was basic text formatting. Now it's time to cover paragraph formatting. This is where you set the indent for a paragraph or make sure that it's double-spaced or that there's enough separation between paragraphs.

In this section we're going to walk through how to change the formatting of a specific paragraph. Once you're comfortable enough in Word, I'd advise that you learn Styles and use those instead. They're discussed in the next chapter.

Alright then. Let's talk about how to format a paragraph one element at a time.

PARAGRAPH ALIGNMENT

There are four choices for paragraph alignment. Left, Center, Right, and Justified. In the image below I've taken the same three-line paragraph and applied each alignment style to it:

> This paragraph is **left-aligned**. I now need to add enough text to this paragraph to make more than one line so you can see the difference between the different alignments. Good times. Especially since I need at least three lines each for you to really see this.
>
> This paragraph is **centered**. I now need to add enough text to this paragraph to make more than one line so you can see the difference between the different alignments. Good times. Especially since I need at least three lines each for you to really see this.
>
> This paragraph is **right-aligned**. I now need to add enough text to this paragraph to make more than one line so you can see the difference between the different alignments. Good times. Especially since I need at least three lines each for you to really see this.
>
> This paragraph is **justified**. I now need to add enough text to this paragraph to make more than one line so you can see the difference between the different alignments. Good times. Especially since I need at least three lines each for you to really see this.

Left-aligned, the first example, is how you'll often see text in documents. The text is lined up along the left-hand side of the page and allowed to end in a jagged line on the right-hand side of the page.

Justified, the last example, is the other common way for text to be presented. Text is still aligned along the left-hand side, but instead of leaving the right-hand side ragged, Word adjusts the spacing between words so that all lines are also aligned along the right-hand side.

For school papers and most work documents you're probably going to use left-alignment. Some places may prefer justified. Books are often published with justified but many do use left-aligned.

Centered, the second example, is rarely used for full paragraphs of text like the main body text of a book. It can be used for sections of text that are only a few lines long such as a quote that starts a chapter. Also, it's often used for chapter or section titles that are then centered over left-aligned or justified text. As you can see, it centers each line and distributes the text for that line equally to the left and right of the center point.

Right-aligned, the third example, is rare. It aligns all of the text along the right-hand side and leaves the left-hand side ragged. I have seen it used for text in side margins of non-fiction books and would expect to see it used for languages that read right to left.

Now that you understand the difference between the options, how do you change the paragraph alignment of your text? As with font, you can do this either before you start typing or by selecting text you've already typed. (For just one paragraph, you can click anywhere in the paragraph, you don't need to select the whole paragraph.)

The way I change paragraph alignment is by going to the Paragraph section of the Home tab and clicking on the image for the alignment type I need in the bottom row of that section.

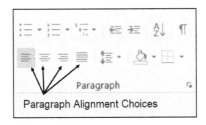

Paragraph Alignment Choices

Each image contains lines that show that type of alignment, but you can also hold your mouse over each one and Word will tell you which one it is.

There are also control shortcuts. Ctrl + L will left-align, Ctrl + E will center your text, Ctrl + R will right-align, and Ctrl + J will justify it. The only one of these I use enough to have memorized is Ctrl + E. I either use left-alignment, which is the default, or I use a Style that includes justifying the text. Since centering is something you do with section headers, I do use that one fairly often.

The third way to change your paragraph alignment is to right-click in your document and choose Paragraph from the dropdown menu. This will give you the Paragraph dialogue box. The first option within that box is a dropdown where you can choose the alignment type you want.

PARAGRAPH SPACING

If you've ever attended school in the United States, you've probably been told at some point to submit a five-page paper that's double-spaced with one inch margins. Or if you've ever submitted a short story you were told to use a specific line spacing. So how do you do that?

As with the other formatting options, you can either do this before you start typing or by selecting the paragraphs you want to change after they've been entered into the document.

Once you're ready, go to the Paragraph section of the Home tab and locate the Line and Paragraph Spacing option. It's to the right of the paragraph alignment options and looks like five lines of text with two big blue arrows on the left-hand side, one pointing up, one pointing down. Click on the small black arrow to the right of the image to bring up the dropdown menu.

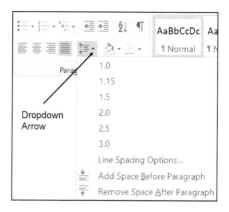

You'll see that you have a choice of single-spaced (1.0) or double-spaced (2.0) as well as 1.15, 1.5, 2.5, and 3.0 spacing. If you want a different spacing than one of those options, then click on Line Spacing Options at the bottom of the list to bring up the Paragraph dialogue box. There you can enter an exact number or choose from even more options.

Generally, the dropdown will be sufficient, though.

Another option, of course, is to just go straight to the Paragraph dialogue box by right-clicking and choosing Paragraph from the dropdown menu. (Just remember to have already selected the text you want to change or to change the spacing before you start typing.)

INDENTING AN ENTIRE PARAGRAPH OR LIST

Sometimes you're going to want to change the starting point of the text on the page. This can be for the first line of a paragraph or for the entire section of text.

When you're dealing with paragraphs, the best way to do this is in the Paragraph dialogue box. Right-click on your paragraph and from the dropdown menu choose Paragraph. Once the Paragraph dialogue box opens, you can set the indent for the entire paragraph as well as whether the paragraph will have a special indent only for the first line.

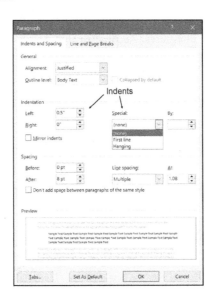

To indent the entire paragraph, change the value under Indentation where it says Left. To indent just the first line of a paragraph, choose First Line from the dropdown menu under Special and then select by how much in the By box. To have the first line flush left, but the lines below that indented, choose Hanging from the dropdown menu under Special and then selected how much those other lines should be indented by entering a value in the By box. (Usually .3 is a good value to go with, Word defaults to .5)

If you just want to indent a line of text or an entire paragraph, you can use the Increase Indent (or Decrease Indent) options in the Paragraph section of the Home tab. These are the ones that have four lines with blue arrows pointing either to the left (for decrease indent) or the right (for increase indent). You can also use tab (to indent) and shift + tab (to decrease an indent).

The problem with the increase indent/decrease indent menu options or the tab keys is in how Word records this for your paragraph format. For example, I just took a single word and indented it using the tab key. Word interpreted this as me wanting that paragraph to be formatted as having a First Line indent of .5". When I instead used the increase indent option on that single word of text, Word interpreted it as Left Indentation of .5". If it's just one line of text, it doesn't matter. But when you're dealing with an entire document, these little discrepancies can become a nightmare.

SPACING BETWEEN PARAGRAPHS

If you choose to style your paragraphs as left-aligned with no first line indent, you're going to need space between your paragraphs. The default style in Word is set up this way. You'll see that as you hit enter for a new paragraph that there's space left between the old paragraph and the new one.

If that space isn't present, you may be tempted to create one by using the enter key. Don't. It will mess with your formatting in a larger document as those spaces you've entered end up at the top or bottom of your pages. It's better to instead format your paragraphs to include the space.

You can do this by selecting your paragraph(s) and going to the Paragraph section of the Home tab. Click on the arrow next to the Line and Paragraph Spacing image (the lines with two blue arrows on the left-hand side, one pointing upward, one pointing downward), and choose Add Space Before Paragraph. In my version of Word that adds a 12 point space before the selected paragraphs.

If you want more control over the spacing around your paragraphs, right-click in your document and choose Paragraph to bring up the Paragraph dialogue box. The third section of the Indent and Spacing tab covers Spacing. On the left side you can see options for Before and After with arrows up and down. You can either type in a spacing value or you can use the arrows to choose the value you want.

If you set your paragraphs to have spacing both before and after, the space between two paragraphs will be the higher of those two values not the combination of them. (So if you say 12 point before and 6 point after, the spacing between them will be 12 point not 18 point.)

If you just wanted spacing at the top of a section of paragraphs or at the bottom of a section of paragraphs, you can click the box to say don't add spacing to paragraphs of the same style. Or you can just add paragraph spacing to that top-most or bottom-most paragraph. Usually this will come into play when you're dealing with a numbered list and want to separate it from the paragraphs of text above and below, but don't want that separation within your list.

If you don't want a space that is there, you can choose Remove Space After Paragraph from the dropdown in the

Paragraph section of the Home tab. If you use this method, just be sure you've selected the correct paragraph (the one before the space you want to remove). Or, you can open the Paragraph dialogue box and change the paragraph spacing values for before and after to zero.

(Paragraph spacing is one of those issues that can become a nightmare in a large document where multiple users have been making edits. This is where using the Format Painter to get the spacing between paragraphs consistent can be a lifesaver. We'll discuss how to use it in the section on Copying Formatting.)

PLACE A BOX AROUND YOUR TEXT

If you want there to be a box around your text (for a resume, for example), you can click anywhere in the paragraph you want a border around, go to the Paragraph section of the Home tab, click on the Borders dropdown, and choose Outside Borders.

PLACE A LINE ABOVE OR BELOW TEXT

You can also use the Borders dropdown to place a line above and/or below your text. Select the text, go to the Paragraph section of the Home tab, click on the Borders dropdown, and choose Bottom Border, Top Border, or both.

PLACE A COLORED BACKGROUND BEHIND YOUR TEXT (SHADING)

You can also add color behind your text. Although they have a similar appearance, this is different from highlighting your text, because this option has a lot more colors available and can also apply to an entire paragraph of text not just selected word(s).

To apply Shading to your text, click on the paragraph or select the text you want shaded, go to the Paragraph section of the Home tab, click on the arrow next to the Shading image (the paint bucket pouring paint), and choose your color from the dropdown menu.

DISPLAY TEXT IN MULTIPLE COLUMNS

If you look at most magazines or newspapers, you'll see that they use multiple columns on the page. Like this:

This is sample text to show you what multiple columns look like on a page.	You can create a document that has one, two, or three even columns or one where there's a small column to the left or right of your main text.	It can be pretty handy to use if you need to put text elements side-by-side.

You can convert your text into two or three columns using the dropdown menu under Columns in the Page Setup section of the Page Layout tab. All you do is select your text and then choose how many columns you want.

If you click on More Columns in the Columns dropdown, this will bring up a Columns dialogue box which allows you to have up to nine columns on the page and to specify the width of each column separately. It also allows you to place a line between each of the columns.

If you add columns to your document, all of the text will continue down the entire page in the left-most column before moving to the next column on the page and all the way down that column before moving to the next column after that.

If you don't want that—if you want the new column to start with a specific sentence instead—you can use section breaks or column page breaks to force the columns to break where you want them to.

Also, I'll just note here that I tend to use tables for something like this instead of columns. I prefer the level of control I have with tables, but it does require more manual placement of the text than the columns option which can be applied to an entire document in less than a minute.

STYLES

Alright. Time to discuss a formatting option that is much easier to work with than paragraph-by-paragraph formatting but that requires a little bit of effort to set up: Styles.

Styles allow you to create a pre-set paragraph format. You get to specify the font, font size, line spacing, text color, whether the paragraph is indented or not, if there's a space between that paragraph and those around it, etc. You can then apply this style to every single paragraph in your document so that they all look the same.

When I format an ebook or paperback, I use two main styles. One is for the first paragraph of a section and has no indent. The other is for all other paragraphs in the document. It's identical to the first style except the paragraph is indented. I will also sometimes use a style for chapter headings. (The CreateSpace template I mentioned previously uses one for chapter headings. In ebooks I usually use Heading 1 for chapter headings.)

Word by default uses a style called Normal. In my version of Word that style uses the Calibri font in an 11 point size with left-aligned paragraphs, a line spacing of 1.08, and a space of 8 points after each paragraph. It also includes widow and orphan control.

Word also provides a number of other Styles that you can choose from. You can see them in the Styles section of the Home tab. Here are the first five:

Each one is formatted to show what it looks like when used and you can right-click on any style and choose Modify to see exactly what formatting it uses. I generally don't like the default styles. I don't need blue italicized text and if I'm going to bold something I can do that with Ctrl + B. The only default styles that really matter to me are Heading 1 and Heading 2. This is because I use them for document navigation while I'm writing and I sometimes use them for inserting a table of contents.

The real power in using styles is creating your own. It only takes setting them up once and then you can apply them in all of your documents going forward to create a consistent appearance both within the document in question and across all of your documents.

The easiest way to create a custom style is to take one paragraph and format it exactly how you want it. Select the paragraph and then click on the arrow with a bar at the bottom of the Styles box on the right-hand side to expand the Styles selections. This will bring up the option to Create a Style.

Click on that option and name your style. When you click on OK the new style will be added to your list of style options, generally in the first row of choices. If it turns out the style that was created wasn't exactly what you wanted, you can right-click on the style and choose Modify. This will bring up the Modify Style dialogue box.

The most common attributes you'll want to change are included on the main screen of the dialogue box, but you can also click on the Format option in the bottom left corner and bring up dialogue boxes for font, paragraph, etc.

Be careful if you leave a style linked to the Normal style like I have in this example. Any changes you make to the Normal style may also impact this style. (A reason I don't modify my Normal style.)

Also, you can choose to either have the style you've created available in only this document or to make it available in all other documents.

(I'm weird so I limit a style to the current document and then use Format Painter to transfer the style to a new document when it's needed. I discuss how to use that in the next chapter, but in general to use Format Painter to bring a style into a new document, select the paragraph in the old document that has the style you want, click on Format Painter, go to your new document, and select a paragraph in the new document where you want to apply the style. This should add the style to your style menu and change the formatting of the text you selected.)

To apply a style from the style menu to text it's as simple as clicking into the paragraph that you want to have the style and then clicking on the style. If you hover your mouse over a style, the text you've selected will change to the new style but it won't remain the new style unless you click on the style.

If you want to convert text of one style to another style, right-click on the name of the current style and choose Select All from the dropdown. Once Word has done that—it may take a bit if it's a long document—click on the new style you want to apply to those paragraphs.

You can also right-click on a style and choose Select All and then modify the style. The changes you make to the style will apply to all instances of the style as long as you've selected them. (It isn't automatic that changes to a style apply to all paragraphs that are already using that style.)

There you have it. Pretty simple, but very powerful. Now one last trick, how to copy formatting.

COPYING FORMATTING

There are going to be times where you've already formatted part of your document or you have a document that's formatted in the way you want and you want to "copy" that formatting to another portion of your document or a different document. This is where the Format Painter tool comes in handy. It's located on the Home tab in the Clipboard section.

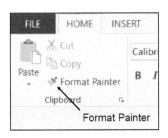

It's especially useful for copying paragraph formatting because it will copy not only basic formatting like the font, font size, color, bolding, underline, italics, etc. but also the paragraph spacing and indent. Often in my corporate career I was able to use the format painter to fix a document when nothing else worked.

If you want to take formatting from one set of text and use it on another, first select the text with the formatting you want. Next, click on the Format Painter image. Finally, select the text you want to copy the formatting to.

A few tips.

You need to use the mouse or trackpad to select the text you want to have the formatting. Using the arrow and shift keys doesn't work.

You'll know that the format painter is ready to paint the format when you see a little paintbrush next to your cursor as you hover over your document.

You can sweep formatting that's in one document to another document.

Format painting can be unreliable if there are different formats in the sample you're taking the formatting from. For example, if I have a sample where part of the text is red and part of the text is bolded and I format sweep from that sample to new text, only the formatting of the first letter in my sample will carry over.

Sometimes with paragraph or numbered list formatting, I have to select the paragraph from the bottom to the top instead of top to bottom in order to get the format painter to carry over the formatting I want. And sometimes I need to select more than one paragraph to sweep from in order to get the line spacing to carry over.

Last but not least, when you copy formatting over, all of the formatting in your target text will be removed. This can be an issue if you've used italics or bolding within a paragraph, for example. Maybe you want the paragraph spacing and font and font size from another document so you use the format painter. Problem is, any bold, italics, or underline in the text you're copying the formatting to will be lost.

There is a way in newer versions of Word to find all italicized text in a document. Same with bolded or underlined. So you could format sweep and then go back to a prior version of the document, locate the italics, bolding, and underlining, and manually put them back into the document now that it has the new formatting. It all depends on which option will be easier.

In summary, while the format painter is incredibly powerful and I use it all the time, you also need to be cautious in how you apply it so that you don't inadvertently introduce errors or erase formatting you don't want to erase. Sometimes it's the only way I can get paragraphs to look the same. Nothing else will do it. So learn this tool. It *will* save you at some point or another.

CONCLUSION

So that's the basics of text and paragraph formatting in Word.

If you get stuck, reach out at:

mlhumphreywriter@gmail.com

I'm happy to help. I don't check that email account every single day but I do check it regularly and will try to find you the answer if I don't know it.

Good luck with it!

APPENDIX A: BASIC TERMINOLOGY

TAB

I refer to the menu choices at the top of the screen (File, Home, Insert, Design, Page Layout, References, Mailings, Review, View, Developer) as tabs. If you click on one you'll see that the way it's highlighted sort of looks like an old-time filing system.

CLICK

If I tell you to click on something, that means to use your mouse (or trackpad) to move the arrow on the screen over to a specific location and left-click or right-click on the option. (See the next definition for the difference between left-click and right-click).

If you left-click, this selects the item. If you right-click, this generally creates a dropdown list of options to choose from. If I don't tell you which to do, left- or right-click, then left-click.

LEFT-CLICK/RIGHT-CLICK

If you look at your mouse or your trackpad, you generally have two flat buttons to press. One is on the left side, one is on the right. If I say left-click that means to press down on the button on the left. If I say right-click that means press down on the button on the right.

Now, as I sadly learned when I had to upgrade computers and ended up with an HP Envy, not all track pads have the left- and right-hand buttons. In that case, you'll basically want to press on either the bottom left-hand side of the track pad or the bottom right-hand side of the trackpad. Since you're working blind it may take a little trial and error to get the option you want working. (Or is that just me?)

SELECT OR HIGHLIGHT

If I tell you to select text, that means to left-click at the end of the text you want to select, hold that left-click, and move your cursor to the other end of the text you want to select.

Another option is to use the Shift key. Go to one end of the text you want to select. Hold down the shift key and use the arrow keys to move to the other end of the text you want to select. If you arrow up or down, that will select an entire row at a time.

With both methods, which side of the text you start on doesn't matter. You can start at the end and go to the beginning or start at the beginning and go to the end. Just start at one end or the other of the text you want to select.

The text you've selected will then be highlighted in gray.

If you need to select text that isn't touching you can do this by selecting your first section of text and then holding down the Ctrl key and selecting your second section of text using your mouse. (You can't arrow to the second section of text or you'll lose your already selected text.)

DROPDOWN MENU

If you right-click in a Word document, you will see what I'm going to refer to as a dropdown menu. (Sometimes it will actually drop upward if you're towards the bottom of the document.)

A dropdown menu provides you a list of choices to select from.

There are also dropdown menus available for some of the options listed under the tabs at the top of the screen. For example, if you go to the Home tab, you'll see small arrows below or next to some of the options, like the numbered list option in the paragraph section. If you click on those arrows, you'll see that there are multiple choices you can choose from listed on a dropdown menu.

DIALOGUE BOX

Dialogue boxes are pop-up boxes that cover specialized settings. As just mentioned, if you click on an expansion arrow, it will often open a dialogue box that contains more choices than are visible in that section. When you right-click in a Word document and choose Font, Paragraph, or Hyperlink that also opens dialogue boxes.

Dialogue boxes allow the most granular level of control over an option. For example, the Paragraph Dialogue Box has more options available than in the Paragraph section of the Home tab.

(This may not apply to you, but be aware that if you have more than one Word document open and open a dialogue box in one of those documents, you may not be able to move to the other documents you have open until you close the dialogue box.)

CONTROL SHORTCUTS

I'll occasionally mention control shortcuts that you can use to perform tasks. When I reference them I'll do so by writing it as Ctrl + a capital letter. To use the shortcut just hold down the control key while typing the letter specified. Even though the letter will be capitalized, you don't need to use the capitalized version for the shortcut to work. For example, holding down the Ctrl key and the s key at the same time will save your document. I'll write this as Ctrl + S.

ABOUT THE AUTHOR

M.L. Humphrey is a former stockbroker with a degree in Economics from Stanford and an MBA from Wharton who has spent close to twenty years as a regulator and consultant in the financial services industry.

You can reach M.L. at mlhumphreywriter@gmail.com or at mlhumphrey.com.

www.ingramcontent.com/pod-product-compliance
Lightning Source LLC
LaVergne TN
LVHW052316060326
832902LV00021B/3932